A MESSAGE TO GARCIA

*Visit our website for more of
the greatest success guides ever written*
WWW.SUCCESSBOOKS.NET

As a Man Thinketh by James Allen
Think and Grow Rich by Napoleon Hill
The Science of Getting Rich by Wallace D. Wattles
The Way to Wealth by Benjamin Franklin
The Art of War by Sun Tzu

A MESSAGE TO GARCIA

And Other Essential Writings on Success

ELBERT HUBBARD

EDITED BY
CHARLES CONRAD

BEST SUCCESS BOOKS

❡ "Get your Happiness out of your Work ✦✦ or you'll never know what Happiness is!" ✿✿

CONTENTS

Aphorisms of Elbert Hubbard
scattered throughout

ELBERT HUBBARD

INTRODUCTION

A *Message to Garcia* has been printed and reprinted more times than any other piece of literature in the history of the world—the Bible excepted. It has been translated into some forty to fifty languages and dialects—and the end is not yet in sight.

Hubbard describes his inspiration so: "The immediate suggestion came from a little argument over the tea cups when my son Bert suggested that Rowan was the real hero of the Cuban War. Rowan had gone alone and done the thing—carried the message to Garcia!

"It came to me like a flash! Yes, the boy is right, the hero is the man who does the thing—does his work—carries the message. I got up from the table and wrote *A Message to Garcia*."

The *Message* was first printed in the March, 1899 issue of the *Philistine*; it ran without a headline, so little did Hubbard think of it. But when orders and re-orders poured in—when the entire issue of that *Philistine* was exhausted in three days—there was naturally some wonder as to what had created the interest.

"What is it that has stirred things up?" asked Hubbard of one of the boys.

"It's that stuff about Garcia," he replied.

Then George Daniels of the New York Central Railroad asked for a price on one hundred thousand copies—rush. The Roycrofters' printing facilities were so limited, they estimated it would take two years to get out the order. So instead, they gave Mr. Daniels permission to reprint it in his own way.

The New York Central promptly issued an edition of one hundred thousand copies, which were promptly snatched up. Then four more editions were issued by them of one hundred thousand each—and then an edition of half a million. Then more and more, until everybody lost count. Millions!

The *Message to Garcia* officially opened the Twentieth Century—for Elbert Hubbard, for the Roycrofters, and for American Business.

Up to that time, I venture that Hubbard still thought of himself as "retired" and of the Roycrofters as an incident to his retirement. After the *Message* was blazoned on the sky Hubbard visioned his future. He decided to be the Voice of American Business.

There are thousands of American writers who can write entertainingly, interestingly, on arts and letters, but the romance of business is on their blind side. Given a business subject, they easily prove themselves writers, only writers and nothing but writers. Their grasp of business is nil.

Yet in this country and century there is no romance that touches the lives of so many people as does the romance of business. Here, business and the business of living are the same thing.

Hubbard had scored two distinct successes, as a business-man and as a writer, so had an extraordinary advantage. The average writer has no knowledge of business, no sympathy with it; often only a contempt. And the average businessman, once he takes his pen in hand, is often inarticulate.

First, last, and all the time, Hubbard was a business-man. He liked to think and speak of himself as such: "I am a businessman with a literary attachment." Freely he gave his admiration to the man who had to "look a payroll in the eye."

He knew the problems of business. He felt he knew the solution to some of them. Therefore, when he spoke-up he spoke authoritatively. *A Message to Garcia* was the first of a series of essays on business problems, which, when placed in the proper hands, have helped to lighten the burden on the businessman's shoulders.

Inevitably, these sane, sound, practical articles attracted the attention of executives everywhere—raised the question, "Who is this man Hubbard?"—and quickly doubled the circulation of the *Philistine*.

Hubbard's style was so lucid, his illustrations so natural, his logic so absolute, that whoever read the *Message* or its companion essays found business an absorbing subject and training a pleasant exercise.

He taught non-readers to enjoy reading.

He taught non-thinkers to think.

He easily convinced the top executives that here was one writer who was practical—who was not an irresponsible know-nothing—and who was well worth a businessman's time.

Here follows *A Message to Garcia*, written one night by the Sage of East Aurora.

—FELIX SHAY
Elbert Hubbard's Personal Assistant
1925

A MESSAGE TO GARCIA

As the cold of snow in the time of harvest, so is a faithful messenger to them that send him: for he refresheth the soul of his masters. —PROVERBS 25:13

IN ALL THIS CUBAN BUSINESS there is one man stands out on the horizon of my memory like Mars at perihelion. When war broke out between Spain and the United States, it was very necessary to communicate quickly with the leader of the Insurgents. Garcia was somewhere in the mountains of Cuba—no one knew where. No mail or telegraph message could reach him. The President must secure his co-operation, and quickly. What to do!

Some one said to the President, "There is a fellow by the name of Rowan who will find Garcia for you, if anybody can."

Rowan was sent for and was given a letter to be delivered to Garcia. How "the fellow by the name of Rowan" took the letter, sealed it up in an oilskin pouch, strapped it over his heart, in four days landed by night off the coast of Cuba from an open boat, disappeared into the jungle, and in three weeks came out on the other side of the Island, having traversed a hostile country on foot, and delivered his letter to Garcia— are things I have no special desire now to tell in detail. The point that I wish to make is this: McKinley gave Rowan a letter to be delivered to Garcia; Rowan took the letter and did not ask, "Where is he at?" By the Eternal! there is a man whose form should be cast in deathless bronze and the statue placed in every college of the land. It is not book-learning young men need, nor instruction about this and that, but a stiffening of the vertebrae which will cause them to be loyal to a trust, to act promptly, concentrate their energies: do the thing— "Carry a message to Garcia."

General Garcia is dead now, but there are other Garcias.

No man who has endeavored to carry out an enterprise where many hands were needed, but has been well-nigh appalled at times by the imbecility of the average man—the inability or unwillingness to concentrate on a thing and do it.

Slipshod assistance, foolish inattention, dowdy indifference, and half-hearted work seem the rule; and no man succeeds, unless by hook or crook or threat he forces or bribes other men to assist him; or mayhap, God in His goodness performs a miracle, and sends him an Angel of Light for an assistant. You, reader, put this matter to a test: You are sitting now in your office—six clerks are within call. Summon any one and make this request: "Please look in the encyclopedia and make a brief memorandum for me concerning the life of Correggio."

Will the clerk quietly say, "Yes, sir," and go do the task?

On your life he will not. He will look at you out of a fishy eye and ask one or more of the following questions:

Who was he?

Which encyclopedia?

Where is the encyclopedia?

Was I hired for that?

Don't you mean Bismarck?

What's the matter with Charlie doing it?

Is he dead?

Is there any hurry?

Shall I bring you the book and let you look it up yourself?

What do you want to know for?

I wasn't hired for that anyway!

And I will lay you ten to one that after you have answered the questions, and explained how to find the information, and why you want it, the clerk will go off and get one of the other clerks to help him try to find Garcia—and then come back and tell you there is no such man. Of course I may lose my bet, but according to the Law of Averages I will not.

Now, if you are wise, you will not bother to explain to your "assistant" that Correggio is indexed under the C's, not in the K's, but you will smile very sweetly and say, "Never mind," and go look it up yourself.

And this incapacity for independent action, this moral stupidity, this infirmity of the will, this unwillingness to cheerfully catch hold and lift—these are the things that make pure Socialism unworkable. If men will not act for themselves, what will they do when the benefit of their effort is for all? A first mate with knotted club seems necessary; and the dread of getting "the bounce" Saturday night holds many a worker to his place.

Advertise for a stenographer, and nine out of ten who apply can neither spell nor punctuate—and do not think it necessary to.

Can such a one write a letter to Garcia?

"You see that bookkeeper," said a foreman to me in a large factory.

"Yes; what about him?"

"Well, he's a fine accountant, but if I'd send him up-town on an errand, he might accomplish the errand all right, and on the other hand, might stop at four saloons on the way, and when he got to Main Street would forget what he had been sent for."

Can such a man be entrusted to carry a message to Garcia?

We have recently been hearing much maudlin sympathy expressed for the "downtrodden denizens of the sweat-shop" and the "homeless wanderer searching for honest employment," and with it all often go many hard words for the men in power.

Nothing is said about the employer who grows old before his time in a vain attempt to get frowsy ne'er-do-wells to do intelligent work; and his long, patient striving with "help" that does nothing but loaf when his back is turned. In every store and factory there is a constant weeding-out process going on. The employer is continually sending away "help" that have shown their incapacity to further the interests of the business, and others are being taken on.

No matter how good times are, this sorting continues: only if times are hard and work is scarce, the sorting is done finer— but out and forever out the incompetent and unworthy go. It is the survival of the fittest. Self-interest prompts every employer to keep the best—those who can carry a message to Garcia.

I know one man of really brilliant parts who has not the ability to manage a business of his own, and yet who is absolutely worthless to any one else, because he carries with him constantly the insane suspicion that his employer is oppressing, or intending to oppress, him. He can not give orders; and he will not receive them. Should a message be given him to take to Garcia, his answer would probably be, "Take it yourself!"

Tonight this man walks the streets looking for work, the wind whistling through his threadbare coat. No one who knows him dare employ him, for he is a regular firebrand of discontent. He is impervious to reason, and the only thing that can impress him is the toe of a thick-soled Number Nine boot.

Of course I know that one so morally deformed is no less to be pitied than a physical cripple; but in our pitying let us drop a tear, too, for the men who are striving to carry on a great enterprise, whose working hours are not limited by the whistle, and whose hair is fast turning white through the struggle to hold in line dowdy indifference, slipshod imbecility, and the heartless ingratitude which, but for their enterprise, would be both hungry and homeless.

Have I put the matter too strongly? Possibly I have; but when all the world has gone a-slumming I wish to speak a word of sympathy for the man who succeeds—the man who, against great odds, has directed the efforts of others, and having succeeded, finds there's nothing in it: nothing but bare board and clothes. I have carried a dinner-pail and worked for day's wages, and I have also been an employer of labor, and I know there is something to be said on both sides. There is no excellence, per se, in poverty; rags are no recommendation; and all employers are not rapacious and high-handed, any more than all poor men are virtuous.

My heart goes out to the man who does his work when the "boss" is away, as well as when he is at home. And the man who, when given a letter for Garcia, quietly takes the missive, without asking any idiotic questions, and with no lurking intention of chucking it into the nearest sewer, or of doing aught else but deliver it, never gets "laid off," nor has to go on a strike for higher wages. Civilization is one long, anxious search for just such individuals. Anything such a man asks shall be granted. His kind is so rare that no employer can afford to let him go. He is wanted in every city, town and village—in every office, shop, store and factory.

The world cries out for such: he is needed, and needed badly—the man who can carry A MESSAGE TO GARCIA.

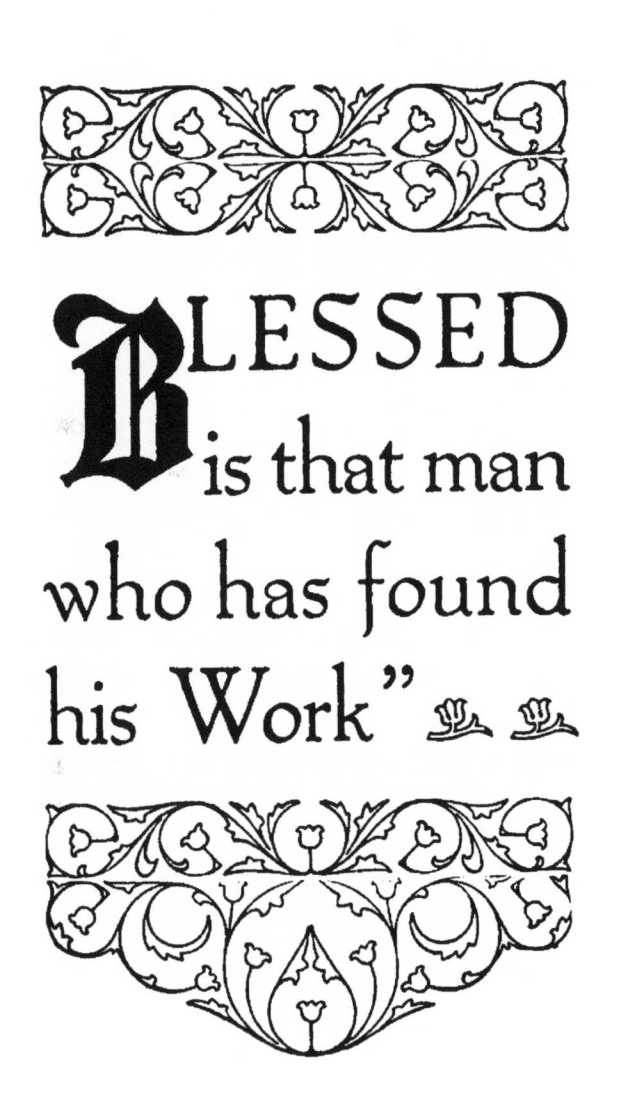

BLESSED is that man who has found his Work"

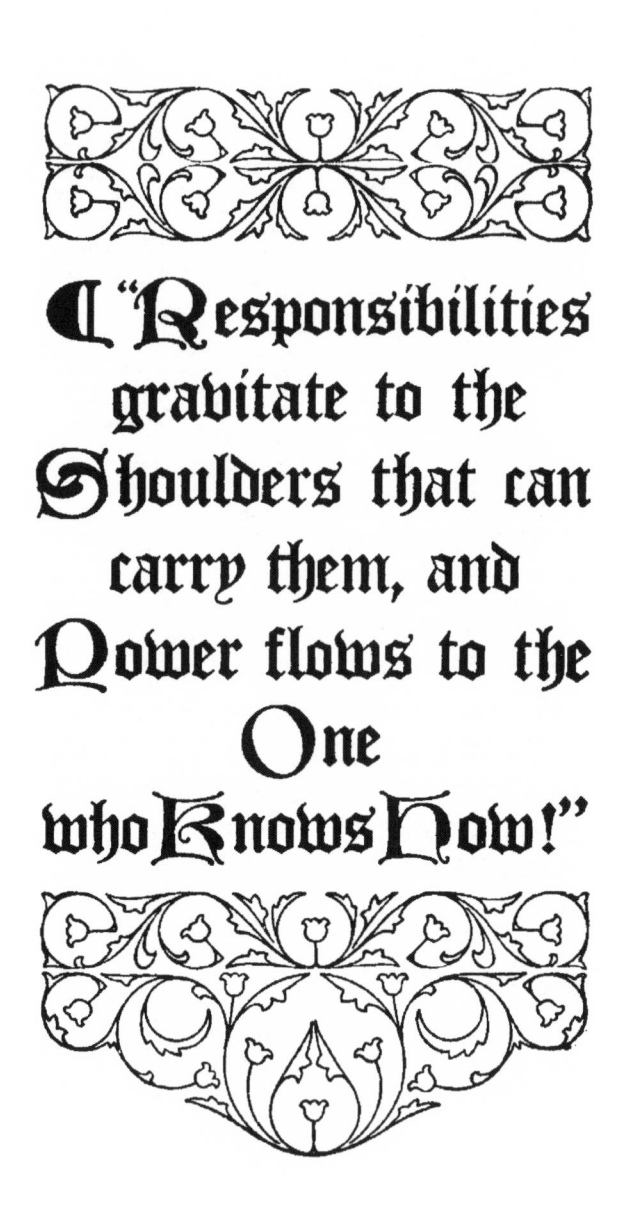

❧ "Responsibilities
gravitate to the
Shoulders that can
carry them, and
Power flows to the
One
who Knows How!"

A LETTER
FROM LINCOLN

Abraham Lincoln's letter to Hooker! If all the letters, messages and speeches of Lincoln were destroyed, except that one letter to Hooker, we still would have an excellent index to the heart of the Rail-Splitter.

In this letter we see that Lincoln ruled his own spirit; and we also behold the fact that he could rule others. The letter shows wise diplomacy, frankness, kindliness, wit, tact and infinite patience. Hooker had harshly and unjustly criticized Lincoln, his commander in chief. But Lincoln waives all this in deference to the virtues he believes Hooker possesses, and promotes him to succeed Burnside. In other words, the man who had been wronged promotes the man who had wronged him, over the head of a man whom the promotee had wronged and for whom the promoter had a warm personal friendship.

But all personal considerations were sunk in view of the end desired. Yet it was necessary that the man promoted should know the truth, and Lincoln told it to him in a way that did not humiliate nor fire to foolish anger; but which surely prevented the attack of cerebral elephantiasis to which Hooker was liable.

Perhaps we had better give the letter entire, and so here it is:

Executive Mansion, Washington, January 26, 1863.

Major-General Hooker:

General:—I have placed you at the head of the Army of the Potomac. Of course, I have done this upon what appear to me to be sufficient reasons, and yet I think it best for you to know that there are some things in regard to which I am not quite satisfied with you.

I believe you to be a brave and skillful soldier, which, of course, I like. I also believe you do not mix politics with your position, in which you are right.

You have confidence in yourself, which is a valuable if not an indispensable quality.

You are ambitious, which, within reasonable bounds, does good rather than harm; but I think that during General Burnside's command of the army you have taken counsel of your ambition and thwarted him as much as you could, in which you did a great wrong to the country, and to a most meritorious and honorable brother officer.

I have heard, in such a way as to believe it, of your recently saying that both the army and the government needed a dictator. Of course, it was not for this, but in spite of it, that I have given you the command. Only those generals who gain successes can set up dictators. What I now ask of you is military success, and I will risk the dictatorship. The government will support you to the utmost of its ability, which is neither more nor less than it has done and will do for all commanders. I much fear that the spirit you have aided to infuse into the army, of criticizing their commander and withholding confidence from him, will now turn upon you. I shall assist you as far as I can to put it down. Neither you nor Napoleon, if he were alive again, could get any good out of an army while such a spirit prevails in it. And now beware of rashness, but with sleepless vigilance go forward and give us victories.

Yours very truly, A. LINCOLN.

One point in this letter is especially worth our consideration, for it suggests a condition that springs up like deadly nightshade from a poisonous soil. I refer to the habit of carping, sneering, grumbling and criticizing those who are above us. The man who is anybody and who does anything is certainly going to be criticized, vilified and misunderstood. This is a part of the penalty for greatness, and every great man understands it; and understands, too, that it is no proof of greatness. The final proof of greatness lies in being able to endure contumely without resentment. Lincoln did not resent criticism; he knew that every life was its own excuse for being, but look how he calls Hooker's attention to the fact that the dissension Hooker has sown is going to return and plague him! "Neither you, nor Napoleon, if he were alive, could get any good out of an army while such a spirit prevails in it." Hooker's fault falls on Hooker—others suffer, but Hooker suffers most of all.

Not long ago I met a Yale student home on a vacation. I am sure he did not represent the true Yale spirit, for he was full of criticism and bitterness toward the institution. President Hadley came in for his share, and I was given items, facts, data, with times and places, for a "peach of a roast."

Very soon I saw the trouble was not with Yale, the trouble was with the young man. He had mentally dwelt on some trivial slights until he had gotten so out of harmony with the place that he had lost the power to derive any benefit from it. Yale college is not a perfect institution—a fact, I suppose, that President Hadley and most Yale men are quite willing to admit; but Yale does supply young men certain advantages, and it depends upon the students whether they will avail themselves of these advantages or not. If you are a student in college, seize upon the good that is there. You receive good by giving it. You gain by giving—so give sympathy and cheerful loyalty to the institution. Be proud of it. Stand by your teachers—they are doing the best they can. If the place is faulty, make it a better place by an example of cheerfully doing your work every day the best you can. Mind your own business.

If the concern where you are employed is all wrong, and the Old Man is a curmudgeon, it may be well for you to go to the Old Man and confidentially, quietly and kindly tell him that his policy is absurd and preposterous. Then show him how to reform his ways, and you might offer to take charge of the concern and cleanse it of its secret faults. Do this, or if for any reason you should prefer not, then take your choice of these: Get Out, or Get in Line. You have got to do one or the other—now make your choice. If you work for a man, in heaven's name work for him.

If he pays you wages that supply you your bread and butter, work for him—speak well of him, think well of him, stand by him and stand by the institution that he represents.

I think if I worked for a man, I would work for him. I would not work for him a part of the time, and the rest of the time work against him. I would give an undivided service or none. If put to the pinch, an ounce of loyalty is worth a pound of cleverness.

If you must vilify, condemn and eternally disparage, why, resign your position, and then when you are outside, damn to your heart's content. But I pray you, as long as you are a part of an institution, do not condemn it. Not that you will injure the institution—not that—but when you disparage a concern of which you are a part, you disparage yourself.

More than that, you are loosening the tendrils that hold you to the institution, and the first high wind that happens along, you will be uprooted and blown away in the blizzard's track—and probably you will never know why. The letter only says, "Times are dull and we regret there is not enough work," et cetera.

Everywhere you will find these out-of-a-job fellows. Talk with them and you will find that they are full of railing,

bitterness, scorn and condemnation. That was the trouble—
thru a spirit of fault-finding they got themselves swung around
so they blocked the channel, and had to be dynamited. They
were out of harmony with the place, and no longer being a
help they had to be removed. Every employer is constantly
looking for people who can help him; naturally he is on the
lookout among his employees for those who do not help,
and everything and everybody that is a hindrance has to go.
This is the law of trade—do not find fault with it; it is founded
on nature. The reward is only for the man who helps, and in
order to help you must have sympathy.

You cannot help the Old Man so long as you are explain-
ing in an undertone and whisper, by gesture and suggestion,
by thought and mental attitude that he is a curmudgeon and
that his system is dead wrong. You are not necessarily menac-
ing him by stirring up this cauldron of discontent and warm-
ing envy into strife, but you are doing this: you are getting
yourself on a well-greased chute that will give you a quick
ride down and out. When you say to other employees that the
Old Man is a curmudgeon, you reveal the fact that you are
one; and when you tell them that the policy of the institution
is "rotten," you certainly show that yours is.

This bad habit of fault-finding, criticizing and complain-
ing is a tool that grows keener by constant use, and there is
grave danger that he who at first is only a moderate kicker
may develop into a chronic knocker, and the knife he has
sharpened will sever his head.

Hooker got his promotion even in spite of his many fail-
ings; but the chances are that your employer does not have

the love that Lincoln had—the love that suffereth long and is kind. But even Lincoln could not protect Hooker forever. Hooker failed to do the work, and Lincoln had to try some one else. So there came a time when Hooker was superseded by a Silent Man, who criticized no one, railed at nobody— not even the enemy.

And this Silent Man, who could rule his own spirit, took the cities. He minded his own business, and did the work that no man can ever do unless he constantly gives absolute loyalty, perfect confidence, unswerving fidelity and untiring devotion. Let us mind our own business, and allow others to mind theirs, thus working for self by working for the good of all.

"If you want to get the Work done, select the Busy Man -- the Other Kind has no time!

MENTAL ATTITUDE

SUCCESS IS IN THE BLOOD. There are men whom fate can never keep down—they march forward in a jaunty manner, and take by divine right the best of everything that the earth affords. But their success is not attained by means of the Samuel Smiles-Connecticut policy. They do not lie in wait, nor scheme, nor fawn, nor seek to adapt their sails to catch the breeze of popular favor. Still, they are ever alert and alive to any good that may come their way, and when it comes they simply appropriate it, and tarrying not, move steadily on.

Good health! Whenever you go out of doors, draw the chin in, carry the crown of the head high, and fill the lungs to the utmost; drink in the sunshine; greet your friends with a smile, and put soul into every hand-clasp.

Do not fear being misunderstood; and never waste a moment thinking about your enemies. Try to fix firmly in your own mind what you would like to do, and then without violence of direction you will move straight to the goal.

Fear is the rock on which we split, and hate the shoal on which many a barque is stranded. When we become fearful, the judgment is as unreliable as the compass of a ship whose hold is full of iron ore; when we hate, we have unshipped the rudder; and if ever we stop to meditate on what the gossips say, we have allowed a hawser to foul the screw.

Keep your mind on the great and splendid thing you would like to do; and then, as the days go gliding by, you will find yourself unconsciously seizing the opportunities that are required for the fulfillment of your desire, just as the coral insect takes from the running tide the elements that it needs. Picture in your mind the able, earnest, useful person you desire to be, and the thought that you hold is hourly transforming you into that particular individual you so admire.

Thought is supreme, and to think is often better than to do. Preserve a right mental attitude—the attitude of courage, frankness and good cheer.

Darwin and Spencer have told us that this is the method of Creation. Each animal has evolved the parts it needed and desired. The horse is fleet because he wishes to be; the bird flies because it desires to; the duck has a web foot because it wants to swim. All things come through desire and every sincere prayer is answered. We become like that on which our hearts are fixed.

Many people know this, but they do not know it thoroughly enough so that it shapes their lives. We want friends, so we scheme and chase 'cross lots after strong people, and lie in wait for good folks—or alleged good folks—hoping to be able to attach ourselves to them. The only way to secure friends is to be one. And before you are fit for friendship you must be able to do without it. That is to say, you must have sufficient self-reliance to take care of yourself, and then out of the surplus of your energy you can do for others.

The individual who craves friendship, and yet desires a self-centered spirit more, will never lack for friends.

If you would have friends, cultivate solitude instead of society. Drink in the ozone; bathe in the sunshine; and out in the silent night, under the stars, say to yourself again and yet again, "I am a part of all my eyes behold!" And the feeling then will come to you that you are no mere interloper between earth and heaven; but you are a necessary part of the whole. No harm can come to you that does not come to all, and if you shall go down it can only be amid a wreck of worlds.

Like old Job, that which we fear will surely come upon us. By a wrong mental attitude we have set in motion a train of events that ends in disaster. People who die in middle life from disease, almost without exception, are those who have been preparing for death. The acute tragic condition is simply the result of a chronic state of mind.

Character is the result of two things, mental attitude, and the way we spend our time. It is what we think and what we do that make us what we are.

By laying hold on the forces of the universe, you are strong with them. And when you realize this, all else is easy, for in your arteries will course red corpuscles, and in your heart the determined resolution is born to do and to be. Carry your chin in and the crown of your head high. We are gods in the chrysalis.

"Initiative
is doing
the Right
Thing
without
being
told"

INITIATIVE

THE WORLD BESTOWS its big prizes, both in money and honors, for but one thing. And that is Initiative.

What is Initiative? I'll tell you: It is doing the right thing without being told. But next to doing the right thing without being told is to do it when you are told once. That is to say, carry the Message to Garcia!

There are those who never do a thing until they are told twice: such get no honors and small pay. Next, there are those who do the right thing only when necessity kicks them from behind, and these get indifference instead of honors, and a pittance for pay. This kind spends most of its time polishing a bench with a hard-luck story. Then, still lower down in the scale than this, we find the fellow who will not do the right thing even when some one goes along to show him how, and stays to see that he does it; he is always out of a job, and receives the contempt he deserves, unless he has a rich Pa, in which case Destiny awaits near by with a stuffed club.

To which class do you belong?

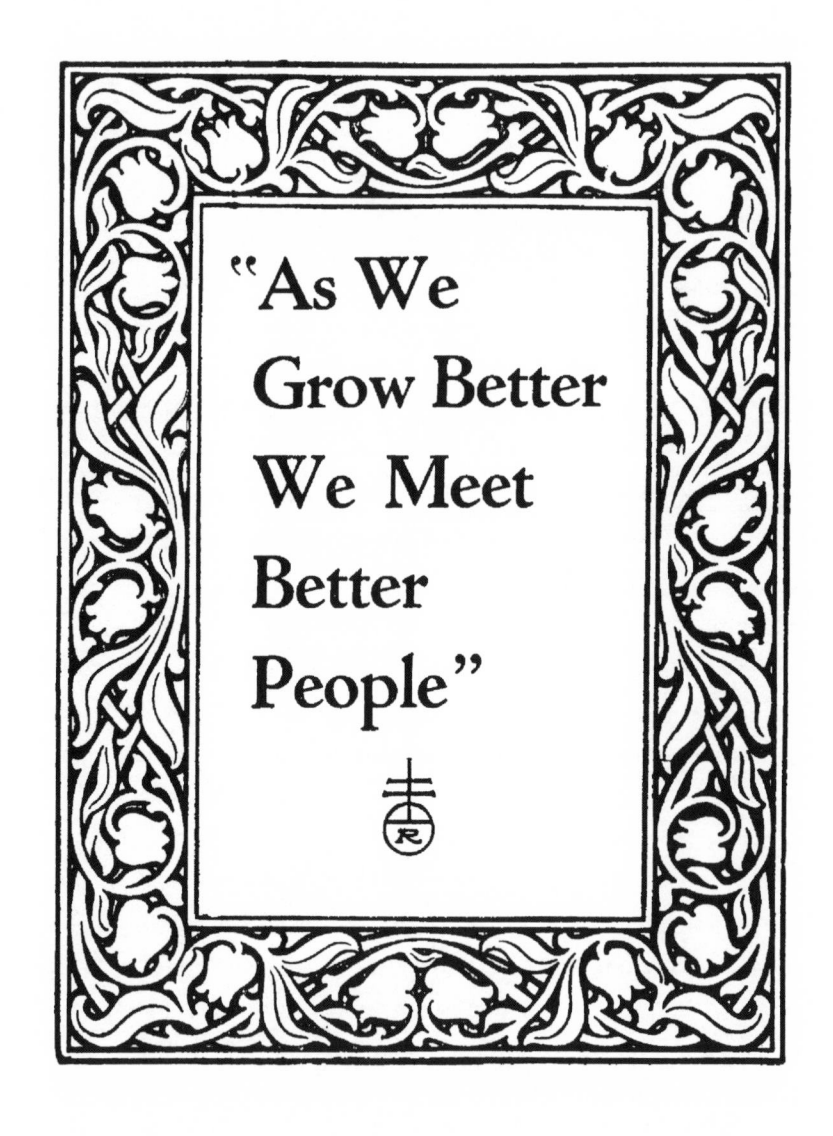

"As We
Grow Better
We Meet
Better
People"

ABILITY

EVERY SUCCESSFUL ENTERPRISE is the result of individual power. Cooeperation, technically, is an iridescent dream—things cooeperate because one man makes them. He cements them by his will.

But find this man, and get his confidence, and his weary eyes will look into yours and the cry of his heart shall echo in your ears. "O, for some one to help me bear this burden!"

Then he will tell you of his endless search for Ability, and of his continual disappointments and thwartings in trying to get some one to help himself by helping him.

Ability is the one crying need of the hour. The banks are bulging with money, and everywhere are men looking for work. The harvest is ripe. But the Ability to captain the unemployed and utilize the capital, is lacking—sadly lacking. In every city there are many five- and ten-thousand-dollar-a-year positions to be filled, but the only applicants are men who want jobs at fifteen dollars a week. Your man of Ability has a place already. Yes, Ability is a rare article.

But there is something that is much scarcer, something finer far, something rarer than this quality of Ability.

It is the ability to recognize Ability.

The sternest comment that ever can be made against employers as a class, lies in the fact that men of Ability usually succeed in showing their worth in spite of their employer, and not with his assistance and encouragement.

If you know the lives of men of Ability, you know that they discovered their power, almost without exception, thru chance or accident. Had the accident not occurred that made the opportunity, the man would have remained unknown and practically lost to the world.

The experience of Tom Potter, telegraph operator at an obscure little way station, is truth painted large. That fearful night, when most of the wires were down and a passenger train went through the bridge, gave Tom Potter the opportunity of discovering himself. He took charge of the dead, cared for the wounded, settled fifty claims—drawing drafts on the company—burned the last vestige of the wreck, sunk the waste iron in the river and repaired the bridge before the arrival of the Superintendent on the spot.

"Who gave you the authority to do all this?" demanded the Superintendent.

"Nobody," replied Tom, "I assumed the authority."

The next month Tom Potter's salary was five thousand dollars a year, and in three years he was making ten times this, simply because he could get other men to do things.

Why wait for an accident to discover Tom Potter? Let us set traps for Tom Potter, and lie in wait for him. Perhaps Tom Potter is just around the corner, across the street, in the next room, or at our elbow. Myriads of embryonic Tom Potters await discovery and development if we but look for them.

Suppose we cease wailing about incompetence, sleepy indifference and slipshod "help" that watches the clock. These things exist—let us dispose of the subject by admitting it, and then emphasize the fact that freckled farmer boys come out of the West and East and often go to the front and do things in a masterly way. There is one name that stands out in history like a beacon light after all these twenty-five hundred years have passed, just because the man had the sublime genius of discovering Ability. That man is Pericles. Pericles made Athens.

And to-day the very dust of the streets of Athens is being sifted and searched for relics and remnants of the things made by people who were captained by men of Ability who were discovered by Pericles.

There is very little competition in this line of discovering Ability. We sit down and wail because Ability does not come our way. Let us search for "Ability," and possibly we can jostle Pericles there on his pedestal, where he has stood for over a score of centuries—the man with a supreme genius for recognizing Ability. Hail to thee, Pericles, and hail to thee, Great Unknown, who shall be the first to successfully imitate this captain of men.

"Men are only
Great
as they
are Kind"

THE GENTLEMAN

SYMPATHY, KNOWLEDGE AND POISE seem to be the three ingredients that are most needed in forming the Gentleman. I place these elements according to their value. No man is great who does not have Sympathy plus, and the greatness of men can be safely gauged by their sympathies. Sympathy and imagination are twin sisters. Your heart must go out to all men, the high, the low, the rich, the poor, the learned, the unlearned, the good, the bad, the wise and the foolish—it is necessary to be one with them all, else you can never comprehend them. Sympathy!—it is the touchstone to every secret, the key to all knowledge, the open sesame of all hearts. Put yourself in the other man's place and then you will know why he thinks certain things and does certain deeds. Put yourself in his place and your blame will dissolve itself into pity, and your tears will wipe out the record of his misdeeds. The saviors of the world have simply been men with wondrous sympathy.

But Knowledge must go with Sympathy, else the emotions will become maudlin and pity may be wasted on a poodle instead of a child; on a field-mouse instead of a human soul. Knowledge in use is wisdom, and wisdom implies a sense of values—you know a big thing from a little one, a valuable fact from a trivial one. Tragedy and comedy are simply questions of value: a little misfit in life makes us laugh, a great one is tragedy and cause for expression of grief.

Poise is the strength of body and strength of mind to control your Sympathy and your Knowledge. Unless you control your emotions they run over and you stand in the mire. Sympathy must not run riot, or it is valueless and tokens weakness instead of strength. In every hospital for nervous disorders are to be found many instances of this loss of control. The individual has Sympathy but not Poise, and therefore his life is worthless to himself and to the world.

He symbols inefficiency and not helpfulness. Poise reveals itself more in voice than it does in words; more in thought than in action; more in atmosphere than in conscious life. It is a spiritual quality, and is felt more than it is seen. It is not a matter of bodily size, nor of bodily attitude, nor attire, nor of personal comeliness: it is a state of inward being, and of knowing your cause is just. And so you see it is a great and profound subject after all, great in its ramifications, limitless in extent, implying the entire science of right living. I once met a man who was deformed in body and little more than a dwarf, but who had such Spiritual Gravity—such Poise—that to enter a room where he was, was to feel his presence and acknowledge his superiority. To allow Sympathy to waste itself on unworthy objects is to deplete one's life forces. To conserve is the part of wisdom, and reserve is a necessary element in all good literature, as well as in everything else.

Poise being the control of our Sympathy and Knowledge, it implies a possession of these attributes, for without having Sympathy and Knowledge you have nothing to control but your physical body. To practice Poise as a mere gymnastic exercise, or study in etiquette, is to be self-conscious, stiff, preposterous and ridiculous. Those who cut such fantastic tricks before high heaven as make angels weep, are men void of Sympathy and Knowledge trying to cultivate Poise. Their science is a mere matter of what to do with arms and legs. Poise is a question of spirit controlling flesh, heart controlling attitude.

Get Knowledge by coming close to Nature. That man is the greatest who best serves his kind. Sympathy and Knowledge are for use—you acquire that you may give out; you accumulate that you may bestow. And as God has given unto you the sublime blessings of Sympathy and Knowledge, there will come to you the wish to reveal your gratitude by giving them out again; for the wise man is aware that we retain spiritual qualities only as we give them away. Let your light shine. To him that hath shall be given. The exercise of wisdom brings wisdom; and at the last the infinitesimal quantity of man's knowledge, compared with the Infinite, and the smallness of man's Sympathy when compared with the source from which ours is absorbed, will evolve an abnegation and a humility that will lend a perfect Poise. The Gentleman is a man with perfect Sympathy, Knowledge, and Poise.

"God will not look you over for Medals, Degrees or Diplomas, but for Scars!"

WORK AND WASTE

THESE TRUTHS I HOLD to be self-evident: That man was made to be happy; that happiness is only attainable through useful effort; that the very best way to help ourselves is to help others, and often the best way to help others is to mind our own business; that useful effort means the proper exercise of all our faculties; that we grow only through exercise; that education should continue through life, and the joys of mental endeavor should be, especially, the solace of the old; that where men alternate work, play and study in right proportion, the organs of the mind are the last to fail, and death for such has no terrors.

That the possession of wealth can never make a man exempt from useful manual labor; that if all would work a little, no one would then be overworked; that if no one wasted, all would have enough; that if none were overfed, none would be underfed; that the rich and "educated" need education quite as much as the poor and illiterate; that the presence of a serving class is an indictment and a disgrace to our civilization; that the disadvantage of having a serving class falls most upon those who are served, and not upon those who serve—just as the real curse of slavery fell upon the slave-owners.

That people who are waited on by a serving class cannot have a right consideration for the rights of others, and they waste both time and substance, both of which are lost forever, and can only seemingly be made good by additional human effort.

That the person who lives on the labor of others, not giving himself in return to the best of his ability, is really a consumer of human life and therefore must be considered no better than a cannibal.

That each one living naturally will do the thing he can do best, but that in useful service there is no high nor low.

That to set apart one day in seven as "holy" is really absurd and serves only to loosen our grasp on the tangible present.

That all duties, offices and things which are useful and necessary to humanity are sacred, and that nothing else is or can be sacred.

A PRAYER

THE SUPREME PRAYER of my heart is not to be learned, rich, famous, powerful, or "good," but simply to be radiant. I desire to radiate health, cheerfulness, calm courage and good will. I wish to live without hate, whim, jealousy, envy, fear. I wish to be simple, honest, frank, natural, clean in mind and clean in body, unaffected—ready to say "I do not know," if it be so, and to meet all men on an absolute equality—to face any obstacle and meet every difficulty unabashed and unafraid.

I wish others to live their lives, too—up to their highest, fullest and best. To that end I pray that I may never meddle, interfere, dictate, give advice that is not wanted, or assist when my services are not needed. If I can help people, I'll do it by giving them a chance to help themselves; and if I can uplift or inspire, let it be by example, inference, and suggestion, rather than by injunction and dictation. That is to say, I desire to be radiant—to radiate life.

WWW.SUCCESSBOOKS.NET
Visit us online for free books and more!

Think and Grow Rich
by Napoleon Hill

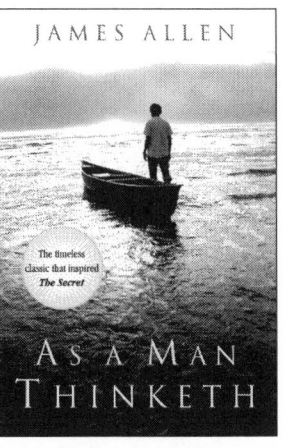

As a Man Thinketh
by James Allen

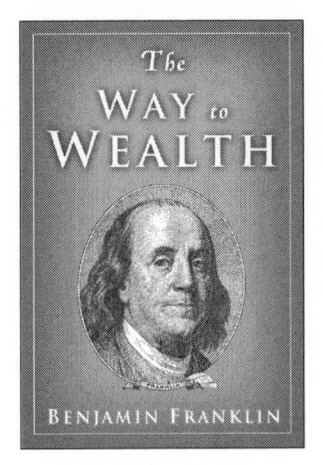

The Way to Wealth
by Benjamin Franklin

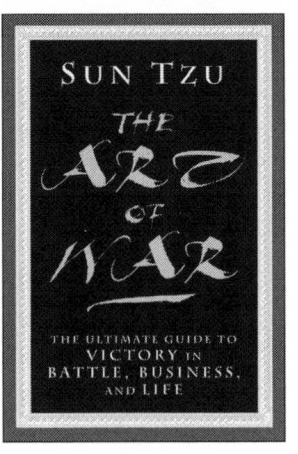

The Art of War
by Sun Tzu

83744357R00028

Made in the USA
Middletown, DE
15 August 2018